Where Do We Go From Here?

Kenneth W. Hagin

—1—

FAITH TO CHANGE OUR DESTINY

We are living in a time when our standard of living is going up, up, up. We enjoy mechanical conveniences and physical luxuries such as the world has never known.

But no other generation that has ever lived on the face of the earth has had as many cares of life as our generation.

Never has any generation faced the perplexing problems we face today. Despite all of our efforts and technological advances, misery is being piled on top of misery. Famine and disease stalk many lands. Mankind, both as a whole and individually, stands in dire need.

I believe, however, that the Word of God teaches that we can change things. The devil may have destined us for pain and sorrow, but we can change our destiny through faith in God.

We hold the key to our own destiny and future. God doesn't. God already has done everything He's going to do for mankind. He has made a way of escape. Through the blood redemption of the Lord Jesus Christ, we can have faith to change our destiny while on this earth.

We have two choices: We can either fold our hands and succumb to complacency, or we can look to the fields that are white unto harvest—to the souls who are lost, dying, and going into sin's hell—to those who are bound by the chains of sickness and disease and need help—and go out and bring them in.

Paul says in Philippians 3, *"Brethren, I count not myself to have apprehended* [you could also use the words to obtain, to excel, to have excelled here]: *but this one thing I do, forgetting those things which are behind, and reaching forth unto those things which are before, I press toward the mark for the prize of the high calling of God in Christ Jesus"* (vv. 13–14).

I want you to see something here. The great Apostle Paul said, "I count not myself to have excelled." Then he went on to say, "But this one thing I do, *forgetting* those things which are behind." That's an interesting statement for this great man of God to make. *Not only did Paul have to forget success, he also had to forget failure!*

As He was penning those words, I'm sure Paul's mind went back to the day he stood outside Jerusalem and held the coats of the men who were stoning Stephen— and encouraged them.

Some of you say, "I have trouble forgetting my past." You never were the catalyst who encouraged the stoning of one of God's chosen. You don't have to forget that. Paul did.

He also had to forget his success on Mars Hill in Athens with the great Greek philosophers. Paul proclaimed to them the great "philosophy" of the Gospel of the Lord Jesus Christ. (It's not a philosophy, but Paul presented it to them in that manner to win them and show them who God is.)

This event was a success in Paul's life. Here was a man from Tarsus, an outpost of the Roman empire. He once was named Saul. Now he is standing on Mars Hill with the greatest philosophers in Greece—and he matches them word for word and argument for argument through the power of God. That's a great success. But Paul had to forget it.

He also had to forget that he started one of the largest churches in history—the Church at Ephesus. If you'll study, you'll find that the church had between 20,000 to 40,000 members! That's a pretty good-sized church!

Yet Paul says, "I count not myself to have done anything (or excelled), but this one thing I do, forgetting those things which are behind." Paul forgot success. He forgot failure. He forgot everything that had ever happened to him in the past because it was his history. It couldn't do anything for him now even if he wanted it to.

RECEIVE GOD'S BEST

Too many of us want to live in the past, feeding off some great meeting we attended. We need to answer the question: *"Where do we go from here?"* Where do we go from this moment on? Do we live in the past, or do we forget the past and go on to the greater things God has for us in the future?

Many people in the Word of God have asked themselves that same question: *"Where do we go from here?"*

Looking in Mark's Gospel we find a man who was sitting at a gate beside the road to Jericho. His destiny had been chosen for him through circumstances. He was blind.

They had no welfare funds then; no vocational training for the handicapped; no braille. Circumstances had relegated Bartimaeus to the lowest of the low—to the very pit and dregs of humanity: to begging.

There he sits beside that road, holding up his little cup.

The dust from the hooves of the animals and the feet of the people walking by settles on his clothes. Many times he smells the food some of them are eating, and his stomach cries out for a morsel of bread.

Still he sits there, waving his cup, hoping perchance a wealthy merchant or landowner will drop in a few coins so that he can make it another day.

One day Bartimaeus hears a commotion. There is a great stir in the air. A large crowd seems to be approaching Jericho.

Bartimaeus grabs hold of the hem of somebody's robe that brushes against him. He shakes it and demands, "What's happening? What's happening?"

They reply, "Oh Bartimaeus, it's just Jesus of Nazareth passing by. Don't get yourself excited. The crowd will be gone in a minute, and maybe even you can get a few coins from them."

And Bartimaeus is faced with this question: "What do I do now? *Where do I go from here?*" He realizes that this is the Man who has been going about doing good and healing all who were sick and oppressed of the devil (Acts 10:38).

He realizes this is his opportunity. What he does from this moment on does not rest in the hands of God; it does not rest in the hands of religious leaders. What happens to him from this moment on rests solely with blind Bartimaeus himself!

The Word of God says, *"Faith cometh by hearing and hearing by the word of God"* (Rom. 10:17). Faith that changes your destiny comes by hearing God's Word. In John's Gospel it says that the Word was made flesh and dwelt among us (John 1:14). And that Word was Jesus Christ.

When Bartimaeus hears that the Word is passing by, faith leaps up in his heart. He asks himself, "Do I sit here and let the crowd go by and maybe accumulate a few coins?

Or do I turn to the only help mankind has ever known? Where do I go from here?"

It doesn't take him long to make up his mind and respond to that question. Jumping to his feet, he screams and hollers, *"Jesus, thou son of David, have mercy on me!"*

The men preceding Jesus go over to Bartimaeus and scold, "Hey, be quiet! Shut up! Don't you know Jesus is coming?" (Isn't it strange that those who are always walking out in front of Jesus want everything to be quiet, and those who are walking alongside Him are rejoicing, praising God, and having a good time?)

MARK 10:48
48 And many charged him that he should hold his peace: but he cried the more a great deal, Thou son of David, have mercy on me.

Faith in God cannot be quieted! When circumstances come in like a flood, the cry of faith will ring out the louder! It says here that Bartimaeus didn't shut up—he cried more loudly: *"Jesus, thou son of David, have mercy on me!"* He screamed it at the top of his lungs.

Yes, Bartimaeus could have done as many people do even today. He could have sat there and said, "All right, Lord. You know my needs. I'm just going to sit here and meditate and project my spiritual thoughts. When they reach You, if You want to bless me, just come over here and touch me. I'm going to sit right here and be quiet. I'm not going to cause any commotion. I know you're supposed to be quiet when Jesus is around."

If that's what Bartimaeus had actually said, he would still be sitting, blind, on that road outside of Jericho!

But because he would not be quiet—*the cry of faith cannot be quieted*—he screamed the louder as he heard Jesus approach: "Jesus, have mercy on me!" And his life was changed.

MARK 10:49–52

49 And Jesus stood still, and commanded him to be called. And they call the blind man, saying unto him, Be of good comfort, rise; he calleth thee.
50 And he, casting away his garment, rose, and came to Jesus.
51 And Jesus answered and said unto him, What wilt thou that I should do unto thee? The blind man said unto him, Lord, that I might receive my sight.
52 And Jesus said unto him, Go thy way; thy faith hath made thee whole. And immediately he received his sight, and followed Jesus in the way.

And there He was—Jesus Christ, the Son of God, the Lord of lords and the King of kings in the flesh, His every step ordered by the Holy Spirit—and *He came to a halt at the voice of faith!*

Bartimaeus had faith. He wanted to change his destiny in life.

See it! See Jesus. See the crowd. See them bringing Bartimaeus to Jesus. Here he comes—this blind beggar. Does he fall down, place his face on Jesus' feet and begin to weep, "O Lord, please help me"?

No, that's the way people think it should be done—that's the way some modern preachers and others would tell you it's supposed to be done—but the Bible says that blind Bartimaeus walked up to Jesus, looked in the direction of that voice that was flowing with love from the Master, and asked straightforwardly, "I want to see, Lord."

And Jesus said, "You've got it!"

Immediately, Bartimaeus began seeing, and it says he began to praise God and follow the crowd. He no doubt threw away that money cup, gave the money he had collected to some other poor man, and said, "Here, take this. I'm going with Jesus." He had made his choice. He hadn't listened to those around him who were trying to discourage him.

If you listen to those around you, they'll keep you in bondage. If you read the Word of God through the colored glasses of tradition, you'll remain in bondage. But if you open your eyes wide to the truth of God's Word, you can change your destiny in life. If your destiny is changed, it will be because you realize the truth of God's Word and get up and walk in it.

Find out what God wants from you, and do it. I challenge you: Receive what God has for you! It belongs to you. Don't let the devil take it away from you.

—3—

'LATER' NEVER COMES

In Luke chapter 17 we find a story of 10 lepers, outcasts from society. One day they heard that Jesus was going to be walking down a certain road. These 10 men asked themselves this question: *"Where do we go from here?* We are bound with this loathsome disease. It is mutilating us and taking us to our graves."

One of them said, "We go to Jesus." So the lepers stood close to the road along which Jesus was passing, and cried out, *"Jesus, Master, have mercy on us"* (v. 13). When Jesus saw them, He told them to go show themselves to the priests.

Then they faced another question—the same one: *"Where do we go from here?"* Jesus hadn't said, "Be healed." He had simply said, "Go show yourselves to the priests." There was no change in their condition; their healing had not manifested.

But, you see, under Jewish law, the priests were the only ones who could pronounce them whole in the eyes of society. As one man, the 10 lepers turned in unison. They did not question for a moment whether they should go to the priests or not. They went, and the Word of God says, *"And it came to pass, that, AS THEY WENT, they were cleansed"* (or healed).

They were set free because they chose to do something with their lives.

The fifth chapter of Mark tells two stories: that of a man who came to Jesus asking prayer for his sick daughter and the story of the woman with the issue of blood.

The woman had spent *"all that she had"* on doctors, seeking to get well, but she got no better, *"but rather grew worse,"* the Bible tells us (v. 26). Then it says, *"When she had HEARD of Jesus . . ."* (v. 27).

She had to answer this question: *"Where do I go from here?"*

She said to herself, "I know what I'll do—I'll go touch His clothes. If I can touch His clothes, I'll be well!"

But when she got to where Jesus was, she found a crowd was surrounding Him. Again she had to answer that question: *"Where do I go from here?* What will I do now? Look at this crowd! Is it worth the struggle to get to Him? Is it worth pushing and shoving through this crowd? Is it worth it? Am I right or wrong?"

How many of you have ever been in her place, where the thing you wanted was surrounded by a crowd? Often we decide, "Oh, it's not worth it. I'll get it later." But most of the time, "later" never comes in the natural. It never comes in the spiritual realm, either.

The woman with the issue of blood made her way through the crowd, touched his clothes, and was instantly healed.

In the meantime, we tend to forget Jairus, who was waiting for Jesus to accompany him to his home, where his daughter lay sick. It was immediately after the great miracle of the healing of the woman that the messenger came, tapped Jairus on the shoulder, and said, "Don't bother the Master any longer. Your daughter is dead. It's all over."

It was almost as if Jesus were reading Jairus' thoughts. Jesus told him, "Only believe. Only believe. All things are possible. Only believe."

At that moment, Jairus had to choose. He had to face the question: *"Where do I go from here?* What do I do? Do I break and run home to my family, or do I just walk along leisurely with Jesus because He said not to fear?"

Jairus made the right decision to take Jesus at His Word. He and Jesus continued on to Jairus' house at a leisurely pace. And what happened? Jairus' daughter was raised from the dead!

Often events happen so quickly that you don't have time to think out a decision; circumstances demand an immediate response.

Only those who know the power and truth of the Word of God can make the right decision at those times and receive what they need from God.

The exhilaration and excitement of the great meetings you've attended won't help when you have to meet the enemy. The only thing that will help you then is how much of God's Word you have hidden in your heart to turn loose on him—not how many songs you can sing or how high you can jump.

"Where do we go from here?" We must forget both the failures and successes of the past and walk on to the higher things of God and His Word.

—4—

HOW TO WIN THE WAR
BETWEEN FLESH AND SPIRIT

I've been preaching since I was 18 years old. I've met many pastors. They're always trying to plan some *program*; they're always trying to put something together to make their church or Sunday School better—programs, programs, programs!

Pastors, it's not *your* programs that will put your church over. Forget your programs! Find out what *God's* program is and use it.

The same holds true for individuals. Find out what God wants. Find out what the will of God is for you. Don't do something just because *you* want to do it. Find out what God's Word has to say about your situation.

Find out what God's Word has to say about some decisions you're going to make in business, too. If businessmen would learn to manage with their heads and their hearts, their businesses would be twice as large.

Learn how to walk with God. Ask God, *"Where do I go from here?"* Quit trying to put *your* plan into action. Put *His* plan into action.

Some will protest, "That's contrary to all the laws of nature and business."

If you know for sure that God told you to do something—even though it seems contrary to natural laws—and you do it, there is no way you can fail, because God never fails.

It comes back to the war between the natural and the spiritual. Anytime you ask yourself the question *"Where do I go from here?"*—anytime you face a crisis—there will be this war between the natural and the spiritual. You'd better be smart enough to do it the way the man on the inside (the inner man) wants it done, or you're doomed to failure.

You see, it's not what "I" want; it's not what "I" desire; it's what God wants.

Yes, I realize that we're talking all the time about the fact that we can have the desires of our heart. The problem with people today is that they are asking for everything and they're not receiving, and it's causing some confusion.

Many saved, Spirit-filled people have heard teaching about the things of faith, but all they know is what the natural man says. They know all the "formulas" and all the faith confessions in their heads, but they're not in their hearts (or spirits), so it's not doing them any good to make those faith confessions.

One reason they're not receiving is that they're not in line with John 15, where Jesus said, *"If ye abide in me, and my words abide in you, ye shall ask what ye will, and it shall be done unto you"* (v. 7). The words are abiding, but they're not abiding in the spirit of man; they're abiding in the natural mind of man.

It's time we realized that we need to forget our desires for cars, money, and success. I believe in prosperity as strongly as anybody.

I dress good; I drive good; I eat good; and I will continue to do so, because God's Word says so. (I don't want anybody to think I'm teaching against faith.)

But the point is, we have become selfish with our faith, heaping blessing after blessing upon ourselves when there is a world out there that is lost, dying, and going to hell, bound in chains of sin, sickness, and disease—and we need to set it free.

God has showed us how to use our faith to get clothing on our backs, food on our table, and other good things of life. Let's take that same faith and use it to bring souls into the kingdom! Let's begin to *confess* souls into the kingdom the way we confess finances, clothing, and food.

Let's ask ourselves the question: "*Where do we go from here?*"

Do we go out to another year of enjoying the good life, getting all the blessings and benefits, while the rest of the world slowly sinks into oblivion?

I say "no." Let's take our faith and maintain a balanced Christian life.

—5—

VICTORY TAKES COMMITMENT

There is a commitment that must be made if we're to go beyond the hilarity and the good things that belong to us. There is a commitment that goes with moving on with God.

I like the story of the three Hebrew children in the Book of Daniel. I think sometimes, however, that we miss their point. They told King Nebuchadnezzar, *"Our God whom we serve is able to deliver us from the burning fiery furnace"* (Dan. 3:17).

Some people get upset with the next statement these Hebrew captives made: *"But if not, be it known unto thee, O king, that we will not serve thy gods, nor worship the golden image which thou hast set up"* (v. 18). In other words, they were saying, "But if not, we're not going to recant anyway."

People will say, "Oh, that's a statement of unbelief." I was praying about it recently, asking the Lord about it, and He said, "Well, I didn't look at it as unbelief. What I saw in it was their commitment. They were saying, 'I'm going to serve God no matter what.'"

If you're going to follow God and go beyond just a good time and good things— if you're going to go into the real battle of soul-winning and setting the world free— it's going to take commitment. (In fact, it's going to take commitment even to walk by faith, because the devil's going to find out if you believe what you say you believe.)

Too many people do not realize what commitment means. Paul writes in the third chapter of Philippians, *"Brethren, I count not myself to have apprehended: but this one thing I do, forgetting those things which are behind, and reaching forth* (v. 13). I'm still discussing commitment. "Reaching forth" involves effort. That's spelled W-O-R-K.

Are you still interested in going on with God? It means work—reaching forth, straining, pushing, striving. For what? For *"the high calling of God in Christ Jesus"* (v. 14).

"I press toward the mark" Paul said. When you're "pressing" to get something, you're putting out energy and effort.

You're going to find out very quickly whether you want to put out the effort to be this kind of child of God or not, because the devil is going to fight you. You're going to find yourself having to make this decision: "Where do I go from here? Do I run back to my security, or do I press toward the mark of the high calling of God in Christ Jesus?"

When you make the decision to go all out with God, the devil's going to scream in your ears. You're going to hear it at night. You're going to hear it when you unlock the office door. You're going to hear it when you're in your office.

That's when you'll find out if you really believe Jesus or not. That's when you'll make up your mind whether you're going to be a failure or not.

There are two directions you can take. One is to press on with God. The second is to run back to something that you know is secure. But you'll never be what God wants you to be if you turn and run. On the other hand, if you press toward the mark and begin to confess who you are in Christ Jesus, things will turn out well for you.

The place in which we all want to live with God is having a good time rejoicing and praising. Did you know that you can live in that place even when every wall seems to be falling in on top of you?

Yes, the walls may feel like they're crashing in on top of you. But even if they don't open up in front of you, the Word of God will become jet propulsioned, and it will propel you over the top! One way or another, you will go over, because you can't go under for going on to victory.

You see, when you make the decision to go with God, and you take the Word and put it down in your heart and then under your feet, you're putting it between you and all the works of the devil. There isn't any place for you to go then but over!